W9-BJK-119

The Snake Scientist

Sy Montgomery

Photographs by
Nic Bishop

Houghton Mifflin Company / Boston

For Tyrannosaurus Rex,

tyrant reptile king of my heart — S. M.

For the Interlake, its people and wildlife — N. B.

Text copyright © 1999 by Sy Montgomery
Photographs copyright © 1999 by Nic Bishop

Library of Congress Cataloging-in-Publication Data

Montgomery, Sy.
      The snake scientist / Sy Montgomery ; photographs by Nic Bishop.
        p. cm.
      Includes bibliographical references.
      Summary: Discusses the work of Bob Mason and his efforts to study and protect snakes, particularly red-sided garter snakes.
      ISBN 0-395-87169-7
      1. Thamnophis sirtalis — Juvenile literature. 2. Snakes — Research — Juvenile literature. 3. Mason, Robert Thomas, 1959–   . — Juvenile literature. [1. Garter snakes. 2. Snakes. 3. Mason, Robert Thomas, 1959–   . 4. Zoologists.] I. Bishop, Nic, 1955–   ill. II. Title.
QL666.0636M65 1999
597.96 — dc21   98-6124 CIP AC

Book design by Chris Hammill Paul

Printed in Singapore

TWP 10 9 8 7 6 5

Thousands
of Snakes

You hear them before you see them. On a quiet day, as you approach
one of the dens at the Narcisse Wildlife Management Area in Manitoba, Canada,
you can hear a rustling like wind in dry leaves.

It's the sound of thousands of slithering snakes.

When you look over the fence into the shallow limestone pit, at first it seems
as if the ground is moving. But it's not the ground—it's 18,000 red-sided garter
snakes!

For about six weeks each April and May, thousands of these harmless snakes awaken from eight months' sleep beneath the earth. They pour out of the pits like water—a river of writhing reptiles. At any of the three big dens here, you can see more snakes at a glance than you could find anywhere else in the world: so many snakes that they are piled two feet deep in places . . . so many snakes that you could pick up ten, twenty, even thirty of them in a handful.

The male snakes emerge first and wait for the females to come out.

Bob Mason and his helpers collect some of the snakes to study.

In fact, people in the pit are doing just that. Look: a seventy-four-year-old woman in a pink knitted cap is picking up snakes and stuffing them into a pillowcase. So are a computer programmer from England, a student from Argentina, a social worker from Chicago, a researcher from Australia—a dozen people in all, who have come here from around the world to work with the snakes.

They're all helping Bob Mason. Bearded, blue-eyed, and smiling, he sits cross-legged in his jeans in the center of the pit, surrounded by squirming snakes. "Thanks!" he says to his assistants when they hand him their pillowcases full of snakes. "That's great!"

Bob's office at Oregon State University is filled with snaky things.

Not everyone would be this delighted to receive sacks of live snakes. But Bob, a zoologist at Oregon State University, has been taking home snakes and frogs and turtles to study ever since he was a kid.

Growing up in Connecticut in a family with three brothers and a sister, he identified the creatures in the woods with field guides, learned about their habits, and made comfortable indoor homes for those he caught. He'd observe the animals for a while, then let them go where he found them—unless the animals freed themselves first.

"They used to get away all the time," Bob remembers. "Turtles and snakes would cruise around the house and turn up in the washing machine! It was rough on my mom."

When he wasn't collecting snakes and turtles, tracking animals through the snow, playing baseball, or riding his bike, Bob watched nature shows on TV. He remembers shows about explorers and zoologists meeting whales and eels under the sea, studying lions and elephants in Africa, tracking grizzly bears in Yellowstone. Bob remembers watching and thinking, "I want to be just like them. I could do that!"

Now, at age thirty-eight, he's known as the Snake Scientist. Back in Oregon, his office door is papered with snake cartoons. The screen saver on his computer shows a red-sided garter. On his left wrist he wears a bracelet his students made for him. Instead of beads, it's made of the tiny backbones of a dead snake they found in the field.

Every spring for the past fifteen years, Bob has flown halfway across the continent to the windswept Canadian prairie to study the red-sided garters. Every time he comes, he's dazzled again by the spectacle.

"This is the most awesome, remarkable sight I've seen in my life!" Bob says. Though garter snakes are among the most common snakes in the world, nowhere else do they gather in numbers like this.

No wonder the snakes of Narcisse have become a tourist attraction. Schoolbuses unload some four hundred kids a day in the spring as teachers bring their classes to see them. Parents come pushing babies in strollers.

"These snakes are tremendous ambassadors to the rest of the world for snakes," Bob says, as he allows a snake to slither from one hand into the other. "They're harmless, cute, and fascinating."

If you come to Narcisse, park guides will tell you the rules of snake den etiquette:

- Be careful where you step. There might be a snake underfoot.
- Don't disturb a big group of snakes or pick up a mating pair.
- Never run or chase others with snakes.
- If you pick up a snake, hold it gently with two hands. Allow it to move freely by letting it slide out of one hand and into the other, like a Slinky.
- Always put snakes back where you found them.

Visitors from Tuxedo Park School.

Holding the snakes is fun.

A second-grader with red hair and freckles holds a wild snake in her hands for the first time. "I used to hate snakes, but now I love them!" she says, delighted with her discovery. "They're soft and not slimy!"

Rick Shine, a snake specialist from Australia, is also delighted to see so many snakes. He's traveled here to help Bob study these animals. "I can see more snakes in a day here than in the course of a three-year field study," he says.

Why are there so many snakes in one place? Snakes, like all reptiles, are cold-blooded creatures whose body temperature rises and falls with the weather. They warm up with the sun and cool down when temperatures drop. In the winter they can't put on warm parkas, so they need to find a place to stay where they won't freeze.

Usually snakes crawl into small holes or basements or barns for the winter. Some dig little burrows beneath the frost line. But here, sixty miles north of Winnipeg, the special geology of the area lets some red-sided garters spend the winter at the world's biggest slumber party.

Two feet beneath the topsoil, this land is made of limestone, a soft rock that is dissolved slowly by streams and rivers to form great underground caves. In places these caves have collapsed, producing rubble-filled sinks shallow enough for snakes to crawl in and out. Some sinks are small, sheltering a few hundred snakes. But the three large dens at Narcisse are big enough for tens of thousands at a time. They pack in so thickly that they're stacked in piles on top of one another.

From September to April, the snakes live in a state of suspended animation called brumation. Their heart rate and breathing slow down. They neither eat nor drink. Their blood gets as thick as mayonnaise. But when the spring sun warms the earth, the snakes begin to push up from under the soil—and an extraordinary drama begins.

The male snakes wake up first. They haven't eaten in eight months. They could slither off to nearby marshes to eat frogs and worms—but instead they wait.

They wait for the females to wake up. The males are eager to mate with them. Sometimes one female will be surrounded by a huge "mating ball" of up to one hundred males—so many that she may be smothered by her suitors.

A female emerges from the earth in spring.

In winter the cold snakes huddle together underground.

Male snakes swarm around a female in a mating ball.

Only one of those males will actually mate with the female. With so many to choose from, how does she select a mate? And how do all the male snakes in the huge mating ball figure out which one is the female? These are just two of many mysteries about the snakes' behavior. After mating, the snakes slither off separately to marshes, sometimes twenty miles from the dens, to spend the summer feasting on frogs. How do they know where to go?

Even more mysterious is how the snakes find their way back to the dens. Researchers know only that the adult snakes somehow return again and again to the same den that they stayed in the year before. Nobody knows where the baby snakes spend their first winter. They are born in the marshes in early fall but don't

go back to the dens until they are two years old—and again, nobody knows why.

Except for the snakes, that is, and they're not talking.

But the snakes in the pillowcases may reveal some of the answers. Some will have their temperature taken and their length and sex recorded and then be set free right away. Others will be released with a temporary stripe of color made with a marker on their bellies or with a silver letter painted on their heads. A few others will be taken to a makeshift field laboratory. They might have to slither through mazes or interact with other snakes in a tentlike "arena" before being released back to the den a few days later.

Bob and his coworkers have devised these experiments to try to answer questions about these snakes in particular as well as about some of the most basic questions in biology.

Bob and his coworkers measure each snake's temperature and mark it. Some of the snake experiments are conducted in colorful arenas.

What can the body temperature of a snake tell us about how animals select mates? How can running a snake through a maze reveal how a garter finds its way back to the same den year after year?

A single measurement or experiment might not give the answer, but it may provide a small and important piece of a big puzzle.

That's what Bob loves about science: "It's really fun," he says, "like a jigsaw puzzle. When a piece fits, it's tremendous."

Bob has made some exciting discoveries. He has found out that snakes use chemicals to communicate with one another. He's found out what the snakes eat (frogs), how far away they can travel (up to twenty miles—and that's a long way to go on your belly!), how long they live (about nine years is average). He's even figured out a way to see how many snakes are in each pit.

But he still hasn't found all the answers. That's why he keeps coming back.

Bob hopes his arena experiments will tell him how snakes select their mates.

Reptile Superheroes

Many people are afraid of snakes. But don't be afraid! You'll miss out on some amazing and mysterious animals. Some people claim snakes are more interesting than dinosaurs—and they aren't extinct.

Both snakes and dinosaurs are reptiles—scale-covered, cold-blooded animals. Lizards, crocodiles, and turtles are reptiles, too. But snakes are perhaps the most unusual and fascinating members of the family: long, thin tubes without legs, eyelids, or ears. And yet snakes are the superheroes of the reptile world, with abilities that other reptiles don't have.

Snakes are agile and quick. African black mambas can slither five miles per hour. Snakes flow across land, climb high into trees, burrow deep into the ground, and swim across marshes, lakes, and even oceans. Some kinds, like the sea snakes that have paddle-shaped tails, swim so well they never come out on land at all. And the so-called flying snakes of Southeast Asia and the East Indies hurl themselves from treetops and glide through the air.

Though snakes have no ears, they sense vibrations with the bones of their jaws that we, with our ears, perceive as sound. With their forked tongues, they "taste" odors, picking up chemical information that leads them along an invisible trail to a

Baby red-sided garters like to eat tadpoles.

frog or a rat or another snake. When a snake flicks its tongue in and out, it is collecting chemical particles and transferring them to a special organ in the roof of the mouth called the Jacobson's organ. If one tip of the forked tongue picks up more particles than the other, the snake knows which direction to follow.

Snakes' abilities seem almost magical. They can swallow prey bigger than their own heads by the incredible feat of unhinging their jaws from their skulls. Some snakes, such as vipers, have evolved poisonous saliva—venom—to kill their prey; others, constrictors like boas and anacondas, literally hug their food to death. Snakes can go for weeks or months without a meal. They can "see" heat with special heat receptors in their heads called pit organs.

And snakes can shed their skin—even the "skin" over their eyeballs. Shedding begins at the lips, and as the snake crawls out of the old skin it turns inside out, sort of like a person peeling off a sweater. If you find a shed skin, the tail points in the direction in which the snake was moving.

No wonder people around the world regard snakes with amazement. Though some people are afraid of snakes, many know better: snakes represented healing to the ancient Greeks and knowledge to the ancient Incas.

Some people fear snakes because they are afraid of what they don't understand. One reason Bob likes to study snakes is *because* we know so little about them. "Snakes are beautiful, fascinating

This boa has swallowed a meal much larger than its head.

Bob studies snakes because we have much to learn from them.

animals who can teach us much about how to live in sometimes difficult situations," he says.

"We know an awful lot about mammals, but much less about reptiles," he continues. One reason we know more about mammals is that we're mammals ourselves. We have hair instead of scales. We feed our babies milk produced from our own bodies. (A baby snake would rather have a worm or a mouse.) And we mammals are warm-blooded, not cold-blooded. Unlike reptiles, we produce our own body heat and keep it constant.

Just because *we're* mammals doesn't mean mammals are any "better" than reptiles, Bob says. Because reptiles are cold-blooded, they can get by with less food—they don't need as much fuel for their internal "furnace." It's a mistake to think that mammals are "more advanced" than reptiles—or even that people are "more advanced" than snakes. True, people have bigger brains than snakes—but we can't shed our skins or see heat or smell with our tongues. It all depends on your point of view.

"And from one basic point of view, reptiles are more successful than mammals," Bob points out. "Look at the Age of Dinosaurs. They were on the earth for 400 million years!" Even today, there are more reptile species (5,970) than mammal species (4,050). There are more than 2,700 species of snakes alone. Snakes first appeared more than 130 million years ago and are now going stronger than ever. "If the last great era of life was called the Age of Dinosaurs," Bob's Australian colleague, Rick Shine, points out, "this era could be called the Age of Snakes!"

Of all the different kinds of snakes, the ones that have spread over the widest range and are most common today are not the venomous vipers or adders, the giant boas or anacondas, but the harmless little snakes such as garters.

Garter snakes live all over North and Central America. Some probably live in your yard or a nearby park. "They're doing *something* right!" Bob says. What's the secret of their success? One way to find out is to study them where their success is most unlikely: at the Narcisse pits.

Think of it: these are cold-blooded animals, yet they're living where it can snow eight months out of the year. "These snakes are living on the edge," says Bob. "This is a harsh environment for a reptile. If they don't make it back to the den in September they won't survive. So the population in this area is unique. The big dens and the mass mating rituals are very special. They provide some unique opportunities to ask some interesting and important questions. What makes them tick? That's what we want to find out."

Snakes are beautiful, fascinating animals.

Outside the rambling prairie house that Bob uses as a makeshift field laboratory in Manitoba, Michael LeMaster, one of Bob's students, is weighing a plastic tub of margarine on a scale. The container's label says "I Can't Believe It's Not Butter!"

You'd *better* believe it's not butter: a red-sided garter snake has just popped its head out through the small hole in the tub's lid.

Each snake is weighed and measured.

The snake flicks its tongue at the student. "Get back in there!" Michael chides, and gently taps the little head back down. The scale adjusts to subtract the weight of the tub, which keeps the snake from slithering away. Michael writes down his measurement.

The house doesn't seem much like a laboratory. But in many ways it doesn't seem like a normal house, either. At the top of the landing to the basement, out of the way of foot traffic, the researchers have carefully piled about a dozen pillowcases full of squirming snakes. Sometimes a writhing bag of them slowly cartwheels down the stairs.

Open the refrigerator and you're likely to find another surprise: often a researcher puts a snake in there briefly. Because the snakes are cold-blooded, the cool makes them sluggish and easier to handle when they are being weighed and measured.

Bob and his students and colleagues dress in jeans and baseball caps instead of white lab coats. But, like scientists everywhere, they are always taking measurements. How long is that snake? How much does it weigh? Is it male or female? What's its body temperature? How many snakes are there at the den this year?

All these measurements, like the tiny dots that make up a newspaper photograph, can eventually form a picture or, like the individual letters in these words, tell a story.

Here in the field you might think a snake scientist would need lots of fancy equipment. But the team keeps it simple: Bob and his colleagues use three portable notebook computers; three

The scientists take measurements and record them very carefully.

short-wave-radio walkie-talkies so they can communicate with each other at different dens; thermometers and thermal probes; tape measures; pens and paper; pillowcases (he buys them in bulk for 80 cents a dozen at the Salvation Army store); and lots of felt-tip markers.

Now it's 9:45, and the gear is all packed up for a day in the field. Everyone heads out of the house to drive to the Narcisse Wildlife Management Area. The yellow grass of the prairie glows in the sun, so Bob knows the snakes will be out.

You wouldn't know where to find them if it weren't for the two-story-high road sign showing a red-sided garter. The prairie, at first, seems an unlikely place for a snake spectacular. It's a muted landscape of stunted trees, low-growing grasses, and pastel flowers. The aspens don't grow tall because their roots can't stretch below the limestone. Their limbs are knotted because of the wind. Direct from the Arctic, the north wind can roar across the prairie at fifty miles an hour. No wonder even the plants hug the ground: yellow wheat grass, prairie sage, thimbleweed, and the lavender prairie crocus, just now in bloom.

The snake team doesn't stop long to look at the flowers, though. Carrying their equipment in backpacks, they can't wait to walk the half-mile or so from the parking lot to the dens and get to work. There's so much to do.

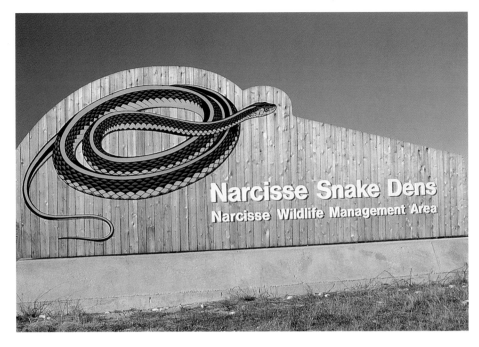

Snake-den sign.

Tiny wildflowers cover the prairies in spring.

21

Collecting snakes.

Crows sometimes peck out a snake's liver.

"If we seem much more mad than even scientists should be," Bob says, "it's because this whole event is over in a matter of weeks. And you can have a week's worth of rain. When the sun is shining, we work like madmen!"

The weather here can change hourly. If it's too cold, the snakes won't come out of the den. Those that are already out may be so slowed by the cold that predators, such as crows, find them easy prey. With so many snakes, the crows can pick and choose the choicest morsels. They often kill a snake to eat only the liver—which they locate with the skill of a surgeon. Or the snakes might just freeze to death. Even in May it sometimes snows.

But today it's sunny, and the snakes at all three dens are active.

The snake team fans out. Along with Bob are two of his students, two other researchers, and six volunteers from an organization called Earthwatch, which provides volunteers to help scientists do fieldwork on projects around the world. With eleven people there are enough to send a group to each of the three big dens.

The first order of business at the middle den is to release some snakes who were captured earlier and used in an experiment yesterday. Today they're none the worse for wear, except for the letters written on their heads in silver paint: S, L, and XL to stand for small, large, and extra-large—just like T-shirt sizes.

Experimental snakes are marked with a number or a letter.

The experiment was like a snake version of TV's *Dating Game.* Each female snake was placed in a tentlike, meter-square "arena" with a choice of several males of different sizes. The results so far suggest that females prefer larger snakes. This result suggests another question, of course: why might larger snakes make better mates?

When the snakes shed their skins, the silver paint will come off, but for the moment, the paint reminds the researchers not to pick up those particular snakes again. They might be tired from the previous capture, and that could bias the results of a new experiment. The freed snakes shoot out of their pillowcases and slither off into the grass.

The snakes are collected in pillowcases, and each one gets a stripe of color on its belly.

Meanwhile, at the south den, Bob is calculating how many snakes there are this year. He dispatches volunteers to collect 500 snakes in pillowcases. "The fun thing about these snakes," Bob says, "is there are so darn many of them you can do a whole experiment in one day. Our colleagues might have to take a whole month just to collect their animals." With the volunteers' help, collecting 500 snakes takes only about ten minutes.

Each of the 500 snakes gets a stripe on its belly in black marker before being released. Thirty-two of them already have blue stripes on their bellies, sixteen of them have red stripes, and four of them have both red and blue. Researchers captured, marked, and released these snakes on two previous days. Bob uses a mathematical formula to calculate the chances that the marked snakes will be among the 500 snakes they have just collected. By counting these snakes he determines how many snakes are probably in that den: he estimates 18,000.

In a mating ball, male snakes pursue the female.

At the north den, another team carefully collects mating balls. At first, right in the pits, it's difficult to tell which snakes are in a mating ball and which ones are simply slithering around. But Bob tells us what to look for: the snakes in a mating ball are clearly gathered around a central attraction, flicking their tongues in and out, rubbing their chins up and down the length of the other snakes' bodies. The male snakes are looking for the female. How do they find her?

That is one of the first questions Bob set out to answer more than a decade ago. Finding the answer changed the course of his research and opened up new questions for researchers studying snakes around the world.

Discovering "Snake Juice"

When Bob first saw the snakes of Narcisse, he was entranced by the mating balls. Flicking black-tipped red tongues, a knot of slithering suitors seethes around the female, rubbing chins up and down her back.

Bob felt sure the males were searching for some clue to tell them which snake was the female. Bob checked off the information the snake could glean from its senses. Could the male snakes see which one was the female? No—from the top and sides, males and females look similar (though the females are usually bigger).

Could they tell by their sense of touch? That was unlikely, too. Males and females feel alike when you touch them: smoother than satin, softer than silk. How about hearing? Snakes can't talk to one another, and if they could, they couldn't hear what the others were saying—they don't have ears. Most researchers believe that

The male polyphemus moth has large feathery antennae to detect pheromones.

snakes don't have the sense of taste as we know it, either. So that left only the sense of smell—a sense that is highly developed in snakes.

Perhaps, when the male snakes rub their chins over the others' backs, Bob reasoned, they are flicking their tongues to detect a chemical "smell" on the skin that will identify the female.

Chemicals that act as signals to influence the behavior or development of other animals of the same species are called pheromones. The word comes from the Greek *pherein,* which means "to carry," and *horman,* meaning "to excite" or "to stimulate." So a snake's pheromone might "carry" a message that would excite or stimulate fellow snakes to behave in a certain way.

Scientists have studied pheromones in a number of different creatures, but mainly in insects. The female silkworm moth, for instance, emits a pheromone that attracts males from miles away when she is ready to mate. But no one had ever found a pheromone in a reptile before.

Pheromones are washed off a red-sided garter snake with soapy water.

So Bob decided to test his idea. First he found a dead female snake and washed her in a bucket of soapy water to remove the natural chemicals from her skin. Both people and snakes have grease on the skin that contains chemicals. We don't feel greasy, but we are: that's why, if you run your fingers down a pane of glass, it leaves a smear. All land animals need this fatty coating to protect our skin from drying out in the air.

Was a pheromone part of the chemical mixture that made up the greasy film on the snake's skin? Bob dabbed some of the material from the soapy water on paper towels to see if male snakes would react.

It worked! The male snakes slithered right to the paper towels — but that was not all. The powerful call of chemistry was so overwhelming that the snakes began to chin-rub and tongue-flick the paper towels exactly as if they were courting a female.

But the experiment was far from over. "So now I've got this juice, but there could be dozens of chemicals in there!" Bob says. How could he determine which chemical was the pheromone?

Bob had studied chemistry in college. He knew he would have to separate out each chemical in the mixture. To do this, he went back to the university laboratory to use a device that looks like a big glass coil, called a gas chromatograph.

As Bob explains, every chemical boils at a different temperature. When a mixture is heated, each chemical comes to its own particular boiling point, then wafts off into the glass coil as a vapor, like smoke going up a chimney.

Chemical after chemical wafted off into the coil. To his dismay, Bob discovered the mixture was far more complex than he'd thought. "I was crestfallen," he said. "There were hundreds of chemicals in there!"

It wasn't the first time Bob had been disappointed. When he was nine years old, he took a career aptitude test in school. Bob had always wanted to be a scientist and study animals, but after the test he was told he wouldn't make a good scientist. Bob was devastated. But his father, a teacher, told him that tests don't know everything. "Ignore the test scores!" his dad said. "Go with your passion!" Even tests are sometimes wrong.

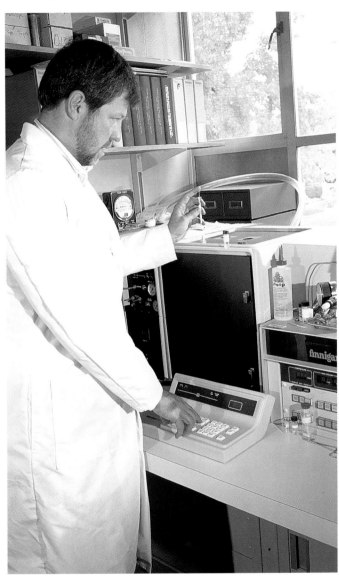

When Bob analyzed his pheromone extract with a gas chromatograph, he found hundreds of different chemicals.

Bob analyzes the extract with a mass spectrometer.

Bob passionately wanted to be a scientist, and he became one. Now, he passionately wanted to find that pheromone. So even though he knew the work would be long and difficult, he took the molecules from the gas chromatograph and ran them through another device, called a mass spectrometer. This device breaks up the molecules even more. It's like a cook working with a recipe, only backward: instead of mixing ingredients together to create a cake or stew, the mass spectrometer breaks down the chemical "stew" into its individual ingredients.

He separated his "snake juice" into hundreds of different compounds, then tested each one on male snakes in his lab. This compound didn't work; that compound didn't work; the snakes ignored one after the other. But finally Bob came up with the right one.

In 1989 he became the first person ever to find a pheromone in a reptile. As often happens in science, finding that answer was the beginning of a whole new story. "That's what's fun about doing science," Bob says. His discovery opened up many new experiments.

The Call of Chemistry

Bob's student Michael kneels in the field beside a plastic container. "OK, guy, let's go," Michael says. A moment later a black-and-yellow-striped head pops out of a little hole cut in the side of the container.

The male snake flicks his tongue in and out. The two forks wave up and down like banners. The snake flows out of the box. He turns left, flicks his tongue, then right, still flicking—hesitant, questing. In a flash, the snake seems to reach a decision. He heads off quickly and purposefully, beelining due south.

A snake follows a pheromone trail laid on the grass.

Michael strides after it, delighted. He had just walked that same route himself minutes before. But it's not Michael's trail the snake is following. It's a chemical trail Michael made by dripping pheromone in a line along the grass.

Michael is following up on his professor's discovery. Bob proved that red-sided garters use a pheromone to detect the presence of females. Now Michael is trying to find out if snakes will follow these chemical signals over land. Can snakes use pheromones to determine which way another snake went?

If they can, it could explain mysteries that have intrigued scientists for decades. Researchers have always wondered how the red-sided garters find the marshes where they feed and give birth in the summertime. They've always wondered how the adults find their way back to their dens in the fall. Perhaps the snakes are following pheromone trails laid on the ground.

These questions don't apply just to snakes. Other animals migrate as well. Many birds, of course, migrate across oceans and continents. Some of the songbirds in your backyard in summer spend the winter in South America. Right whales, humpbacks, and others swim halfway around the globe twice a year. Even some insects migrate. Green darner and globetrotter dragonflies that live in the north spend the winter in warmer places, such as Texas, and monarch butterflies fly from the eastern United States all the way to Mexico, where thousands will settle on a single tree, their orange and black wings outnumbering the tree's own leaves. When a woolly bear caterpillar crawls across the road in the fall, it's migrating too, looking for a place to spend the winter. Scientists still aren't sure how these animals know where to go.

The snakes at Narcisse might offer a good model for understanding how animals migrate. That's what Michael thinks. "The reason it's so good to work with these snakes is that we humans depend on sight, sound, feel—but these guys depend so much on smell. They don't have ears. They can't lift up two meters and look at the horizon. Touch is different—but they can't reach out and grab things. So it's a simpler system." It's easier and clearer to study an animal who's relying mainly on one sense instead of five.

No one knows how the red-sided garter snake finds its way to the marshes.

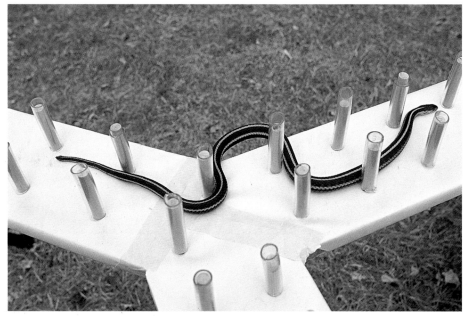

Michael uses a dropper to lay pheromone on the Y-maze.

To test his idea that snakes might be following pheromone trails, Michael first used a simple maze shaped like a Y. The male snake had to pick one leg of the Y or the other. Only one leg had pheromone dabbed on it. Michael tested his maze again and again, using a different snake each time. Sometimes he dabbed pheromone on the right fork, sometimes on the left. The snakes almost always chose the leg with the pheromone trail.

Next Michael moved his experiment to the field. After all, snakes don't live in laboratory mazes. To see if snakes would follow pheromone trails in daily life, Michael tested his idea outside on real grass, where snakes would be likely to encounter such trails.

In this more complicated test, the snake starts out from a container in the middle of a three-meter circle. Now the snake can choose any direction, not just left or right. Would he follow the pathway Michael dribbled out of his eyedropper? Or would the snake take off in a different direction?

Out comes the snake's head. Out flicks the tongue. The snake slithers hesitantly at first, searching. Finally it picks up the trail. To the snake, the chemical trail is as clear as the road markers along a highway. Pheromones, after all, can convey information just as surely as a sign along a road. But instead of "Next Rest Stop 10 Miles," the pheromone says "Female Snake This Way."

Michael sets up an experiment to see if the snakes will follow a pheromone trail on the grass.

Sometimes the snakes form a mating ball in a tree!

That is important information for a male snake. Animals, just like people, are exchanging news, greetings, and information all the time. The howl of a coyote, the white flash of the tail of a fleeing deer, the smile on the face of your friend, all give important information. The coyote's howl proclaims, "I'm a coyote, and I'm over here!" The deer flashes its white tail to say, "I'm running away from something dangerous. Watch out!" And the smile on your friend's face says clearly, but without words, "I'm so glad to see you!"

But snakes can't smile or speak or flash a furry white flag. They use chemicals instead.

The idea that animals signal their fellows with chemicals is fairly new. That's what makes it exciting. "It opens a whole new area," says Michael. "Chemical communication plays a critical role. I'm sure it's going to be found in many species."

In fact, people may have pheromones, too. Recently a researcher working in an American laboratory reported he had found, inside the human nose, a Jacobson's organ like that in snakes and many other animals, including bears and horses. The organ in people is not well developed—no one is even sure it actually works. It might be like our tailbone or appendix:

merely the remainder of a body part that was once important to our long-ago ancestors.

But some new studies suggest that this organ does work—and that perhaps without our even knowing it, our "sixth sense" affects our mood, heart rate, and even our attraction to another person.

There's some good evidence that chemicals in our body fluids may affect the way people around us behave. One group of these chemicals is called androstenes. Even though nobody can smell them, when scientists spray androstenes on seats in a movie theater or waiting room, they find that women are more likely to sit in them—and men are more likely to avoid them.

A California researcher, David Berliner, claims to have identified a dozen different human pheromones. People who sniff these chemicals don't report that they actually smell anything, but Berliner can measure the changes: in response to some pheromones, people's breathing, heartbeat, and body temperature drop slightly. Berliner has even added three of these chemicals to perfumes, and he claims people who wear the perfumes feel more secure and confident.

If it turns out that the Jacobson's organ in people really does work, doctors might one day be able to deliver puffs of pheromone-like drugs to patients to treat ailments ranging from heart disease to mental disorders. But even more intriguing is the possibility that studies of the Jacobson's organ could help us better understand how we behave. Perhaps we are more like snakes than we ever thought!

Who
Needs
Snakes?

Every spring, before Bob visits the Narcisse dens, he and his fellow researchers travel to the nearby town of Inwood. They are making a sort of pilgrimage, to visit a statue built about ten years ago: a statue of two red-sided garter snakes twined in an embrace.

Local people nicknamed the snakes Sam and Sarah. Bob always begins his season in the field by touching the statue. "Maybe they'll bring us good luck," he jokes.

The statue certainly reflects better luck for the snakes. Not too long ago, in the 1930s, these harmless snakes were so feared that public health officials poured gasoline down their dens to kill them.

Most snakes are harmless. Even the most venomous kinds would usually rather retreat than bite. Coral snakes have some of the most poisonous venom, but they are so reluctant to bite people that many nineteenth-century naturalists thought they weren't poisonous at all.

"Snakes are first cowards, next bluffers, and last of all warriors," wrote snake scientist C. H. Pope, who studied some of the most dangerous African snakes. A snake is most likely to slither away before you even get a chance to see it, but if trapped, it might try to make itself look bigger or make a scary sound to get you to back off. That's why cobras spread their hoods, why hognose snakes hiss and puff up, and why rattlesnakes rattle. One snake, the small West Indian ground boa, will even squirt blood from its eyes before it will bite in self-defense.

Still, many people fear snakes so much they try to kill every one they see. Others don't hate snakes, but they don't try to protect them, either: when we build malls or highways on land that snakes need, we rob them of their homes, and that kills them as surely as a bullet or a shovel. Today 200 different species of snakes are in danger of extinction.

The red-sided garter snake tries to strike only when it is threatened.

But the province of Manitoba *celebrates* its snakes! Bob is proud that his work may have helped change people's feelings about snakes. And he's glad that he was able to help the local government make new laws to protect them.

For many years, local people were allowed to take snakes out of the dens and sell them to stores as pets. Bob's snake counts revealed that the population was dropping dramatically every year. His data helped persuade the Canadian government to outlaw snake collecting at the dens.

Park rangers have built a fence and a tunnel so that the snakes do not have to cross the highway.

Now he's working with park officials to help the snakes with another problem. When they leave the dens at the end of May, they must cross busy Highway 17 on their way to the marshes. Thousands are run over by cars. Park officials are now

experimenting with fences that will funnel the migrating snakes into a tunnel dug underneath the road.

Bob considers all this part of his work as a scientist. The snakes have delighted and intrigued him for fifteen years. "Now I want to give some of that excitement and fascination back to the public," he says. "For the people of Manitoba, having the snakes here can give them more joy."

His studies of snakes might one day help people, too. After all, as he points out, "We're actually more similar to snakes than dissimilar. They have all the same organs we do. They have blood. They have lungs. They have hormones." Bob and his colleagues might learn something about snakes that could help us come up with a cure for human disease.

Such discoveries have happened before. Just a few decades ago, researchers around the world were struggling to understand leprosy. This contagious disease, which causes people's skin and bones to rot, was once one of the most terrible afflictions in the world. People who had leprosy were sent away to live in isolated leper colonies so they wouldn't infect other people.

Schoolchildren look into one of the dens.

Everyone wanted to find a cure. A key piece of the puzzle was discovered by a researcher who observed that wild armadillos sometimes got a strange skin disease. It turned out to be leprosy! Armadillos are the only

For Bob, science is exciting and rewarding.

animals other than humans that can get the disease. Thanks to an armadillo scientist, leprosy can now be cured with antibiotics.

Studying snakes could even help people travel in space. Scientists estimate it would take three years to travel to Mars. But there's a big problem: a human can't stay healthy for more than a year without gravity. What if we could sleep those years away, the way snakes do in the winter? Actually, wintering snakes are not asleep but are in a state of suspended animation. Learning more about brumation, as this state is called, might help us come up with a way for astronauts to journey far into the universe.

Paying attention to the wild animals around us helps us keep our planet healthy, too. Animals often show early warning signs that something is wrong in the environment. When populations of bald eagles and other birds of prey declined in the 1960s, scientists discovered that the cause was DDT—a dangerous pesticide that can threaten humans, too. That chemical is now banned, but other dangerous chemicals still pollute our world. In 1995, middle-school students on a field trip in Minnesota discovered hundreds of frogs with missing eyes or with extra legs. Is something in the water responsible? The same water the people drink? Researchers are trying to find out—thanks to the amphibians' tip-off and the observant students.

But what *really* keeps Bob interested in the snakes of Narcisse isn't just the hope of helping humans, though that would be nice. It's something more.

"Humans have a thirst for knowledge," says Bob, "an innate curiosity." And knowledge, he says, is its own reward—like art or music.

Learning about the animals with whom we share this planet offers one way to satisfy our thirst to know. And it satisfies an even deeper need as well.

"The average human feels a shared heritage with other creatures on the earth," Bob says, "and feels a pain when a species vanishes." Without the beauty, surprise, and sheer fun of learning about the living creatures on this planet, he believes, "life would be diminished in a very real sense."

Unsolved Mysteries Many questions remain unanswered about the snakes of Narcisse. Here are just a few that Bob and his team plan to work on in the future.

- Where do the baby snakes, born in August, spend the winter? Why don't they join the adults in the big dens?

- How do older snakes find their way to the dens the first time? Do they spend the winter in their parents' den, or do they select a different one?

- Do snakes use more than one type of pheromone? What other information might pheromones convey?

- Why are male and female snakes different sizes? Why might females prefer bigger snakes as mates?

- How does temperature affect mating behavior? Does it affect males and females differently?

- The fence and tunnel scheme to get snakes safely under Highway 17 has only begun. Many snakes still prefer to cross the road because the asphalt has been warmed by the sun. How can snakes be encouraged to use the tunnels? What are some other ways to protect snakes from cars?

To visit the Narcisse snake dens

The dens are located 130 kilometers north of the city of Winnipeg, on Highway 17. The latter part of April and the first two weeks in May are the best times to visit; the garter snakes return to their dens in early September.

For recorded information on the seasonal status of snake dens, telephone 204-945-6784.

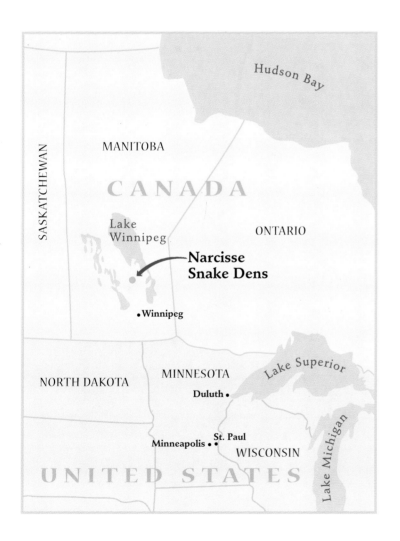

Through the nonprofit organization Earthwatch, ordinary people can help Bob Mason and other researchers with science projects around the world. To learn more about Earthwatch, write:

Earthwatch
PO Box 9104
Watertown, MA 02272

On the Internet, visit *www.earthwatch.org* or E-mail them at *info@earthwatch.org*

For Further Reading

Snakes in Question, by Carl Ernst and George R. Zug (Washington, D.C.: Smithsonian, 1996), answers questions about many kinds of snakes, such as: What is the biggest snake? How does venom work? Can snakes really be charmed?

The Snake Book, by Mary Ling and Mary Atkinson, with photographs by Frank Greenaway and David King (New York: DK Publishing, 1997), is a picture book about twelve kinds of snakes.

I Didn't Know That Some Snakes Spit Poison, by Claire Llewellen (Brookfield, Conn.: Aladdin Books, 1977), tells many amazing facts about snakes.

Outside and Inside Snakes, by Sandra Markle (New York: Simon and Schuster, 1995), describes how snakes hatch, how they hunt, and what their bones, teeth, and organs look like.

Please Respect Snakes

Snakes are fascinating, but unless you are working with a scientist like Bob, you should never disturb them in the wild. Although most snakes are shy, many will bite in self-defense if they feel threatened, and some are poisonous. It is always best to observe wild animals from a respectful distance. They are happiest being left alone.

Acknowledgments Many people (as well as snakes) helped us as we worked on this book. We're very grateful to Bob Mason for explaining and showing us so much and for introducing us to his friends, students, and colleagues. We'd like to thank them, too, especially Rick Shine, Michael LeMaster, Ignacio Moore, Mats Olsson, and Gerry and Al Johnson.

We're grateful to our friends at the Manitoba Department of Natural Resources, particularly Dave Roberts, for taking good care of the snakes and their visitors. We learned a lot from the excellent park interpreters. Thank you, Lisa Avery, Ric Nash, and Colleen Kurlowich.

We also thank our friends at Earthwatch and the volunteers who joined us on our adventure: Ruth Nesbitt, Priscilla Clark, Bill Henderson, Sarah Vinicor, Dave Goodwin, Larry Hum, and Keith Vanning.

For help with writing and editing this book, the author thanks Bob Oksner and our fine editor, Amy Flynn. And finally, we thank our mothers—Audrey Bishop and Willa Zane Montgomery—who, like Bob's mom, put up with our own many adventures in the natural world when we were growing up.

Index